Look Again

Also by Elizabeth Danson

The Luxury of Obstacles

Look Again

POEMS BY Elizabeth Danson

RAGGED SKY PRESS
PRINCETON, NEW JERSEY

Copyright © 2019 by Elizabeth Danson
Published by Ragged Sky Press
270 Griggs Drive
Princeton, NJ 08540
www.raggedsky.com

Text and cover design by Jean Foos
All Rights Reserved
ISBN 978-1-933974-33-0
Library of Congress Control Number: 2019936640
This book has been composed in FF Scala and Joanna MT
Printed on acid-free paper. ∞
Printed in the United States of America

Contents

One

Love mountains | 3
What to Make of It | 4
Can't turn my eyes from it | 5
Undertakers | 7
Resignation | 9
Incident in a Barnyard | 10
Unintended Consequences | 12
Incurable | 13
Empty | 14
Displaced Persons | 16
Ubi Sunt | 18

Two

Processional | 23
Modesty | 24
Some Unfair Complaints | 25
Beeches in April | 26
Everything Is Golden | 27
Birth from Earth | 28
October | 29
Seasonal | 30
Trying Out My Snowshoes | 31
January, Canal | 32
Snowstorm | 33
Winter Wear | 34

Three

Bringing Home the Bacon | 37
Starbaby | 39
Boreal Bravado | 40

At the Bungalow | 41
Knowing When to Leave | 42
When a bear | 44
Duo | 46

Four

Startled | 49
No Fairytale | 50
Life in It | 51
Sea Otters | 52
The fox came back | 53
Light Thrown on Winter Twigs | 54
No View | 55
The Shortest Way | 56
Coming Together | 57
unreadable messages | 58
Countryside Map | 59
Florida | 60
Water Windflower | 61
Orbis Muscae | 62
Perfect Arcs | 63

Five

Surfacing | 67
Dream Strangers | 68
Under Three Skies | 69
Night Cries | 70
Long and Winding Yarn | 71
The Russian doll I played with as a child | 72
Night Thoughts Organized | 73
Many Applicants for One-Way Travel to Mars | 75
Mother Goose Mash-Up | 76
Look Again | 77

Six

The White Horse at Uffington, Oxfordshire | 81
Naming Wildflowers | 83
Dodder [n.] | 84
Witch Hazel | 85
Nettles | 86
Under the Skin | 87
Pole Beans | 88
Unchanged | 89
Winter Trees Are Like Pencil Sketches | 90
Nothing | 91
The Work of a Poet | 92
The Persistence of Myopia in the Human Gene-Pool | 93

Acknowledgments | 95
About the Author | 95

| One

Love mountains

and they'll love you back
I've been hugged
by rocky slopes
grinning with crannies
bearded with moss
slick from recent rain

The first time
I was kissed on the cheek
and stayed black and blue
then greeny-yellow
for weeks

Just a few days ago
it was more
of a full-body embrace
from knee to shoulder
banged up and shredded

In the bathroom mirror
it's clear how close
and intense
our relationship has been—
the mountains and I

What to Make of It

What does it matter
that a space between branches
along the back row of ash trees
closing in my summer yard
holds an upside-down peace sign?
that a bird back there keeps singing
Today? To me? as if amazed at the mail
or the answering machine?

It mattered to my husband's father
that in his final bed he dreamed
over and again of being visited
by Mayor Koch—not the stranger
who intrudes into some dreams
but a personality, a regular visitor;
less disturbing than his late wife
lurking behind the window curtains.

The brain is not mere gray stuff
and will not easily accept *No matter.*
Painted drapery holds monsters, trees,
roads to a place that makes perfect sense.

Can't turn my eyes from it

in news pictures
book titles
at the roadside

even mistaken signs
a work glove
in the gutter looks
like a dead squirrel
or a dropped hoodie
arms outstretched
is a dead dog

a fine grand tree
is beautiful
but the dead ones
in the hedgerow
snag my attention

in the south
where the barns
are shallow and flanged
with side-wings
like tired butterflies
many are deserted

farms abandoned
one-room groceries
emptied out
houses sinking
modestly sideways
or in on themselves
very few posted
for sale

here and there
a drooping gate
shredded curtains
perennials still
in straggly bloom

and everywhere
the kind kudzu
will cover them

Undertakers

Death sends three black vultures
into my part of town
though crows by the half-dozen
are the usual scavengers
that come for a dead squirrel

This doomy-looking triad
approach their task
one by one
with always one guardian
on the nearest rooftop

At first one bird is distracted
by a newspaper
delivered in flesh-colored plastic
but tearing at the cover
lets out only the smell of ink

The business of the team
is dismemberment
and they work
diligently and undistracted
over the course of hours

Grey hooded
they tear through fur
peck flesh
devour guts
leave nothing but a shell

Stiff now
it lies beside the brick path

next to the garbage can
about the size and shape
of a bedroom slipper

One forelimb detached
looks like a chicken wing
picked clean at a cocktail party
from which the black-clad guests
have departed

Resignation

She hangs there, fat,
motionless on the last remaining
laddered triangle of web, dangling
from the tightrope strung
between two bushes. Pounding
rain has washed the rest away,
and not much but gnats
could be caught anymore
without the final rickety contraption
collapsing.

This bright morning might inspire
humans to shake off the lethargy
that came with the first chill rain
of autumn, to hang out linens
or at least to take a walk.
What is she waiting for?
Surely she's ripe
to bursting, a rain-sodden berry,
egg-heavy and ready to die
after a few last rites.

Stoic, unaffected
by the world around her,
she awaits some internal signal
to lay her thousand eggs,
cocoon them in gossamer,
shrink to a nubbin burdened
by her eight legs, once skilled
like a knitter's needles, now
useless, dismiss the view
her many-lensed eyes bring her
of green garden, blue sky,
red twigs, dismantle her life,
give herself to the wind.

Incident in a Barnyard

Prodded again, the pig panics,
swerves sideways, skids
on the dung- and drizzle-slick cobbles—
no easy purchase for her small split hooves.
Men in black rubber boots
mud-smeared to the calves,
soles' deep lugs clogged with straw-stuck manure,
shout into the wind,
wave arms, fists, prodding sticks,
grab for her hot heft in vain;
she shifts her weight, swings around
three pairs of legs, the ramp to the truck
reeking of pig-piss
and a lump of dung still steaming slightly
in the chill March air.

The sow, elusive, trots to the angle
between barn and wall,
turning to face yelling men brandishing staves,
      she is at one with her ancestors
         at bay in the ancient forest hereabouts.
Only a single old elm stands for the rest;
embedded in the lane's dry-stone bank,
it thrusts into the barnyard its bristly bole, budding
with a bundle of tiny clubs, fine brush
for the pig's great sides.
She scrapes herself sidelong against it,
itchy with sweat, upset, but calming now
as the men quiet each other, slow their approach
drop arms and voices.
      Two crows in the elm top
      comment raucously
      hop and jostle for the best branch.

The pig's pink-rimmed eyes
narrow between pale straight lashes,
glance side to side, girlish, at the group approaching;
her tail stiffens, its tuft caught by a twitch of wind.
One man's hand goes to a pocket,
brings out half a turnip, skin purpled like a bruise,
holds out the unexpected gift towards the quivering snout.
She tittups forward, dainty stepping, flirting
with her old friend of the evening fence-chats,
the pocket treats, the scratching behind the ears.
He gives, she takes the turnip, turns her head…

he has her by the ear, seizes her nearest leg,
heaves her bulk sideways; she thuds onto the cobbles,
squeals like a buzz-saw, frantic, kicks out
drawing knuckle-blood with a sharp hoof. Oaths
join the din, shouted injunctions.
Sticks slap against heaving sides, screams
sound her struggle.
Ropes snake out of another pocket. She is hog-tied,
lugged to the truck's ramp, then up it,
into the dark
clanging metallic pen, echoing with pig-cries,
the men's thumping bootfalls, clattering rods. Then
the clanging-to, the locking, the engine's whining roar.
  As the barnyard gate clacks shut
  the wind whips rustling straws
  across the cobbles.
    One of the crows drops
    to peck at a turnip scrap.
    The other clutches his swaying branch,
    shakes ragged feathers into place,
    makes no further comment.

Unintended Consequences

God is so fed up. The world
wasn't meant to turn out like this
when Eden emerged full-blown
from black nothing—peopled
with such a lovely couple
and the pets they named
so inventively: armadillo, shearwater, gnu;
plus the plants and mud puddles
for them to garden with, until
they had to over-reach the permitted grasp
saying *or what's a heaven for?*

But Earth was supposed
to be sufficient, and could have been
if they hadn't started
killing brothers, stealing wives,
considering themselves superior
and therefore allowed
to do anything they felt like.
God, in the end, said
Let there be darkness,
plagues, depression, war,
and whatever else it takes.

Incurable

The world is getting old—a late-summer peach
rotten in at least one spot, the rot bound to spread
until it's through and through. Impossible to excise
the contagion; it reaches to the bitter pit, spoils all.
The tender fuzz, the blush, the flesh-like give, cry out
its desirability, its innocence. *The invisible worm...*
Earth looks beautiful from far enough away—blue,
swirled with pale patterning: watered silk—but come
closer and the oceans suppurate with cast-off garbage,
dead sea-birds, creatures poisoned, tangled in plastic.
The planet is pocked, too, by lethal weapons: gunnery,
slaughterers' knives, and newer—distant, clean-handed—
ways of killing. No cures inoculate against this maggot,
this mildew, the inevitable...*Doth thy life destroy.*

Empty

1.
The robin's-egg-blue shard
is done with, like the shells left
in our breakfast egg-cups,
smeared inside with yolk.

This potential bird
never hatched, nestled, fledged,
nor fluttered after its mother into a bush
shivering its wings and
in that raspy repeated peep
all young birds share, begged
again to be fed.

Maybe it delighted the jay
that scooped it out of its bright shell
to feed nestlings of its own
wearing feathers as blue.

2.
The Shaker Village at Hancock
is a shard of itself:

the practical round barn
fragrant with haydust and pigeons,
crafted from stone and smoothed wood
to shelter the herd for milking;

the gardens for food and medicine,
sweet with lavender,
gleaming with beaded red-currant bushes,
rows of horseradish, marigolds, sage;

the dwelling house like a Rorschach test,
men's side mirroring women's side
and all things simple, plain, pure:
tables, chairs, beds, coat-peg boards;

the workshops for oval boxes, candles, jugs,
ingenious machines for manufacturing pills,
seeds for next year's gardens and for sale,
tools and wheelbarrows stored by size.

And in all the fervor
of creation and labor and prayer,
of singing and holy shivering and shaking,
their celibate purity emptied the village.

Displaced Persons

In search of forage, a new source
of water, wood, or richer tribes to plunder,
our ancestors moved on; hungry, greedy,
or under orders from the chief, they picked out
what wouldn't overburden pack animals
or a flimsy boat—food that would stay edible,
if not good, for weeks: dates, dried fish, biltong,
ship's biscuits, also water containers,
straw raincloaks for shelter.

Now it's a choice of what fits
into an overhead rack, on plane or train
or overcrowded bus. Books and family photos
are too heavy, some clothes too light
for a rumored winter. Familiar foods cannot
pass customs inspection, are abandoned
along with language and the mind's furniture.

I left behind in my parents' attic
paintings I'd made in school art classes,
not good enough to frame but remembered
for the struggle they entailed—how to depict
a foreshortened foot, what color to use
for the leaves of dead cow-parsley—art rolled
in dusty bundles, waiting to become rubbish
at their next move.

The bride has to go
to her husband's compound in return
for the bride-price, learning her in-laws'
favorite foods and how to prepare them, leaving
behind her own childhood—a tree
whose patterned shadows she knew
like the lines on her palm, a sweet-seller

who watched her grow up, remembered her
likes and dislikes, didn't frighten her.

Refugees sent from war fronts by fiat
or violence scrabble through belongings
to choose portable essentials—a knife, shoes
that will walk far, a marriage certificate,
the extra clothes that will delay
having to appear in rags and look
possessionless.

Ubi Sunt

Where are the boys who used to sleep in this twin-bedded room,
burdened with the stuff of their lives—the small model boat, labeled $4,
ping-pong paddles and balls, and the books they read at bedtime,
all *$2 unless marked otherwise*. Clothes in the open almost-emptied closet,
a blue blazer, and one in a madras check, half a dozen dress shirts,
a few short ties, pairs of shoes and white high-tops.

And in the room along the hall the bed has girl things—little purses
of faux leather and pink plastic, strings of beads, a stuffed dog, broken-
necked judging by its posture and its price, *$3*. A princess outfit and
a witch's hat, three naked dolls, various vintages, the oldest perhaps
passed down from a grandmother—cloth body, molded limbs and head
with staring eyes still brown and eyelash-rimmed. Just above its sexless
groin the price on the blue tape reads *$8*—wishful thinking, based on
the *Antiques Roadshow*?

Downstairs in the ranch house
the owners sit in their breakfast nook,
telling all comers *Half Price Today*.
It's been a long weekend of listening
to comments carelessly spoken loud
enough for them to hear: *Horrible
set of dishes; Someone in the family
must have done these paintings—
and such cheap frames! Would you
believe how many mismatched glasses?*
And strange queries: *Does this pitcher
come in a larger size? No ice bucket?*

Great Stuff Downstairs says the sign with an arrow to the basement,
but the pool table's dinged and faded, the skateboard's lost a wheel,
and the tackle box overflows with rusty paint-dulled lures, fishhooks
tangled and bent. There's a curious long-handled black metal trident,
too small to spear a fish worth catching, and a pole topped with a basket

just the size for harvesting plums or peaches, but this house has no
fruit trees, only two dying dogwoods, a back hedge of arborvitae chewed
to deer height, and a front yard that lost its lawn to dirt, moss and
listless pachysandra.

Where are the traces of all those games of catch that happened here,
the first attempts at roller skating, hula hoop spinning, bike riding?
Who but the two sitting in the breakfast nook remember the green station
wagon they drove up in, baby in the back along with suitcases of clothes
and the best china they couldn't trust to the movers? Where are all
the photos of birthdays, holidays and graduations going to go when
they finally move out of here?

Two

Processional

When three turtles take themselves
out of the mess of black mud and leaf-mold
where they've whiled away the winter
they shamble slowly in dirt-splotched shells
out of a deep ditch and down the little drop
into the ice-chilled clutter of the canal
with its bits and bobs of broken branches
looped with lost fishing line and lures
snagged plastic bags and stranded rags
wadded weeds and shadowy willows
that leave pools of light where logs
make platforms for the paddling plodders
to scramble onto and sunbathe side by side
spelling spring to those who spot them.

Modesty

The star magnolia buds start to crack open,
with almost two weeks to go until April.
It will send cinnamon-scented winds across the garden
as I do my flower-bed spring clearing. It will
weather frosts as its more elegant cousins all over town
can't, without each petal turning limp and brown.
Beneath it grow three bush-honeysuckles
already in bloom among dead-looking twigs,
the flowers creamy white like stubborn knuckles
holding out secret prizes to be guessed at. Bee-bags
swollen with pollen on a sunny morning, show
the trove isn't my private pleasure—the bees know.
These signs of earth's tilting turn are sure but quiet
unlike splashy crocuses everywhere running riot.

Some Unfair Complaints

What new can a poet say about April?
We know it's the cruelest month, but why?
Is it the constant weather reverses that
have us craning our necks at the sky
from moment to moment, wishing we had
our umbrellas when slate-grey overtakes
that blue we took for promise of a fine day,
while the temperature drops and makes
us huddle into our collars and pockets, and
scurry toward car or store or home at a run
ready to complain that we thought spring
had finally arrived and with it the blessed sun?
Or is it the speed with which each treat is whisked away—
crocuses, daffodils, blue scillas—none of them will stay.

Beeches in April

Now in the beech woods last year's clinging leaves
that winter faded through derivatives
of autumn's brass and copper shades—pale tea,
yellowing parchment, antique lace—let go,
ceding through primogeniture their right
to new leaves shivering with sap and light.
Nature's first green here isn't gold at all,
nor silver, copper, bronze or shaken foil;
it's green's dream of itself, just as the leaf
is shaped as simply as a child's first stiff
crayoned rendition of the leaf of dreams.
Around the smooth grey trunks fan gracious limbs
as in a formal dance of sylvan gods,
or still, when no wind stirs the sunlit woods.

Everything Is Golden

On a soft evening as April contemplates May
the solid sky breaks up, letting the sun through
as it slides toward the closing of a day
of clouds and cool breezes, bright with new
blossoms and leaves, but not benign
as some of our April days have been this year.
A curious light draws me outside, a sign
of something that makes the precise season clear:
it is the time before a universal green
will fall over the trees like a cargo net;
each has its color, its underlit glow, the scene
is like one skillfully managed for a stage set
where a portentous encounter must be planned
to warrant this eerie light across the plain domestic land.

Birth from Earth

They breech-birth themselves into air
after rootling their way, brown torpedoes,
through the dirt where they've been at home
for so long that air must be baffling, light
piercing, even moon- or starlight, the first
to reach their crimson blood-bead eyes.

Wriggling upward, still swaddled tight
in the final carapace of the old life,
they cling, vertical, for the second birth,
the split shell and the tumbling forth
to hang upside down, soft and vulnerable
until they're strong enough to flip

and dangle by two claws for all the work
of hardening and transformation. Ghost-
pale at first, pigmented only in the eyes
and the black shoulder blades, pivots
for the whirring wings of maturity,
they hang from their old dead bodies.

The rumpled network of veins unfolds
as wings change from dead flower petals
to transparent skeleton-leaves; color comes
to bleached body and legs, and the brief
air-life begins.

October

These mornings just before the first frost, chill
with foresight, air's too heavy for the bee
to traffic in, leaving her clamped and still
on yesterday's last blossom, until she
thaws from her seeming death when a sunbeam
softens her stiffened limbs, stiffens her wings
and sends her foraging where zinnias gleam
among the shadows, while the house wren sings
from reddening dogwood branches, and the last
faint crickets buzz and whisper in the hedge
or underneath the sills where they have passed
the night stuporous as the bee, at the same edge
between revival and the endless curl
into a knot they're powerless to unfurl.

Seasonal

Although it's sonorous, the word Autumn
lacks the forthright simplicity of Fall.
One brings to mind a seasonal hymn,
        Latinate, a bit solemn.
The other's a call
backward to its opposite, when all
is not fall-of-the-leaf
        but spring-into-life.

Strange how resistant living things seem
        to giving in. Flowers dream
of going on forever, new blooms each day
for the visiting insects and the birds that prey
on them, the spiders that build and rebuild
webs to catch late gnats and flies that gild
their bodies as brightly as they did in May.

Yesterday hummingbirds swarmed
all the red and orange blossoms, warmed
by stronger sunshine than the season calls for
part of this perfect Autumn that my spirit falls for.

Trying Out My Snowshoes

I see a mirror child, rosy-cheeked and tired from outdoor play
when I come in from the dazzle of snowshoeing across fields
traced by parallel trails left by skiers, tracks of dogs, footprints
of deer and squirrels, and the embroidery of hopping birds.

Trees outlined in white, old nests with ostrich eggs of snow,
weeds throwing shadows of seedpods and crumpled leaves.
I wished for water, shed gloves, wondered at paths trodden
onto the snow-covered lake—geese? gulls? rabbits mistaking it
for a wide new meadow? I could picture them venturing out
under the night's slim moon between departing snow clouds.
          Perhaps an owl feasted in the spot where a circlet
of rusty feathers on the white sheet told of a robin that stayed
north this winter—weakened by hunger for worms? or just a large
dark target without spring's leafy cover. Wood pigeons I otherwise
wouldn't have noticed took off in a flap of wings and alto
exclamations. A wren tried to sit invisibly still in its tangle
of rose twigs, until I was close enough to touch it.

Mostly, though, I had the blue and white afternoon
to myself. Others had rushed out into the bright morning, hard
to resist. I waited until my return would be at teatime,
as all those years ago when pink cheeks were pinched and kissed.

January, Canal

A late winter this year,
but finally a freeze on the canal
patterned by wind and currents
and the cold coming off the banks.
Some slabs of ice hang
from dangling branches just above
the water—broken windowpanes
over a shatter of crystal. Other
smithereens cluster where they fell.
Cubist shapes etched in the ice
are matched by passages
of expressionist splash and splatter
pierced by fallen twigs,
waterside weeds, rushes, bits
and pieces of ruined canoe docks.

A fisherman on the bridge
casts into a place of running water
between ice stretches, his brown dog
beside him, gray-muzzled, used to it.
Further, in another ice-clear place,
a pair of ducks paddle in shadow,
not mallards—too big, and plain
and dark, none of those dazzling
head feathers on the male, the female's
mottling. At home, my Peterson
tells me *American Black Duck*.
Next day, two feet of snow.

Snowstorm

Snowlight extends the daylight
of a late winter afternoon
growing cold in a heatless house
Fall of flakes riveting
despite their monotony

Occasional odd sounds
in a world without traffic
or even dog walkers
     a thump
might be a snow clump
dropping from a rooftop
or an overburdened bough
     a crack
could be a laden branch
giving way and falling
into the white duvet of snow

Flashlights
and hurricane lantern
gathered in readiness
for the approaching dark

Then
the judder
of the furnace
as sudden light
obscures the shining snow

Winter Wear

Heron at the edge of open water—
ice fisherman, black friar
standing solitary, stark
against snow-cloaked lake ice.

So unknowingly visible
on this bright white afternoon,
plumage designed for camouflage
against waterside earth and twigs.

Snowshoe hare, snowy owl
change into winter wear,
and stoat transforms into ermine
with only that black-tipped tail

to give it away, to make it
desirable as fur trimming
for the gowns of noblemen
and royalty in winter palaces.

Three

Bringing Home the Bacon

Women provided the salad, the cabbage soup,
the starchy stuff that filled them up
day after day—taro or yams or winter gourds,
potatoes roasted in the embers, corn in all
possible manifestations. Children came home
with berries and mushrooms, and mothers
sorted them to pick out the poisonous ones.

When the vegetables were farmed—seeds
saved, ground tilled, hoed for weeds, watered—
then the food harvested (think of the heaviness
of the basket supported by a tumpline
across the brow or balanced by a baby
on the opposite hip) and kept from rotting
by trial and error, ingenuity, women's lore
(some plants had to be dried, some pickled,
some cooked then sealed under wax or oil),
it was the band of women and girls who did it.

The men hunted. They spent hours honing
arrow points and spear points, learning
to follow spoor and what to expect of the prey
at different seasons, times of day, and arc
of the moon. They danced chase and kill,
then left in bands, sometimes for long stretches
and not always to return successful and proud.
But when they brought back meat, even
if only small game, the meals were occasions
for lip licking, marrow sucking, tale telling
about the stalk, the ambush, the slaughter.

Nobody made paintings of the women
carrying water, plying digging sticks,

cooking the daily bread on the hot griddle-stone.
The men sitting in the talking place day by day
between hunts were the ones who mattered.
They brought home the deer, the monkey,
the buffalo or wallaby, the wild boar for bacon.

Starbaby

She was born fully clothed,
swam into the world wearing a scarlet lycra
long-sleeve, snap-crotch body stocking
with plunging neckline and double-frilled cuffs,
and over it, a black suede mini skirt
just long enough to cover those snaps,
with heart-and-flower cutouts all around the hem.
On her feet were black Doc Martens,
size 00, knotted with double bows
to deal with the slippery conditions, and in her hair—
the first thing to appear—a rhinestone star.

Arriving at kindergarten on her Harley Davidson,
she tethered the bike to the chimney
and forgot about it.
When she'd learned to spell ain't and boots and cycle,
to read *Ant & Bee, Alice in Wonderland,* and *Huck Finn,*
she went to go home,
mounted the Harley,
revved and roared off up the road
taking the schoolhouse with her,
teacher hanging out the window,
getting ready to slap the erasers.

She got a job with the phones—
stringing the new lines, fixing them after winter storms,
or hollering loud enough to get the message through,
above gale, against blizzard, between raindrops.
Then one midsummer night,
when she was perched cross-legged on top of a pole,
a bundle of wires in each hand, one in her teeth,
the lightning struck.
She stood up for a moment, one arm raising its crackling torch
like the Statue of Liberty except shucked by the fire,
and left this life stark staring naked.

Boreal Bravado

After the coldest night, even unhoned by birdsong
the morning air is sharp and clear as ice shards.

Climbing the gilded dome of the Czarina's palace
he finds its ice-film crazed in a pattern like the veins
on her hard white breast.

He reaches the zenith and spreads chapped hands
burning with chilblains, to clasp the tiny cupola
invisible from below.

On the narrow parapet he melts with his breath
the rime that veils the polished marble wall.
His pulse thuds

and the shrinking and growing of that patch
of stone un-iced before his lips almost convinces him
it throbs at his touch.

Crabwise he circles to the sunny side, blinded
by frosted glare and flashing wings, sudden thrum of air
as the imperial dovecotes waken.

Hoofs ring and clatter on the far cobbles,
cleared between snowbanks for the safer exercising
of the Czar's horsemen.

When the white borzois burst from the kennels,
their purposeful barking, sharpened by distance,
charges the air he gulps.

The city steams around the palace, a warm body
freshly roused among its covers, those dark furs
the surrounding forests.

Here his exploit ends. He wants to shout to her,
dares not even raise his arms in triumph.

At the Bungalow

In the after-monsoon calm, birdsong again.
They loll on the verandah, she sniffing
at the crisp air, he puffing
a cheroot. A hummingbird visits the vine
where the first bougainvillea blossoms are ruffling

their collars and cuffs. She watches
the tiny jeweled flame flick
shimmering from sip to sip; its quick
purposeful flight mesmerizes her, catches
an inward chord, an inflammable wick.

A vision startles her; he sees her smile
and wonders why: her loins are burning
as she gives rein to the yearning
aroused by the bird's zeal,
its rapt energy, its never turning

from the passionate probing of each flower.
She envisions herself tied with silken bonds
to the verandah hammock, by feet and hands,
naked and rouged where the nether lips flare,
anointed with honey there, that sends

the hummingbird insane. It cannot help
but come to her sweet calyx, hover, dip
over and over that flickering tip
of a tongue into her, to gulp
a strange new nectar, sip by sip.

Closing her eyes, she arches and quivers;
he's turned away, distracted; the travesty
of his voice asking, "Where's the ashtray?"
then, finding the bird gone, she shivers.
He says, "Who's doing cocktails on Saturday?"

Knowing When to Leave

I was one of Eve's best friends. She told me
I was easier to talk to than Adam, or the snake,
which kept hanging around from the branches
of the pomegranate trees that grew all down the valley
where they lived after they left the garden. It
(she never could tell what sex it was) ignored
the command to crawl on its belly and eat dust,
even though Adam followed orders
and threw stones at it whenever he didn't have
his stick in hand to aim at its grinning head.

There was Lilith, of course, but she and her gang
weren't great conversationalists. They excelled
in shimmying their flimsy skirts at Adam,
which Eve couldn't do with her aprons of pelt
or fig leaves, according to the season. I'd never
felt at home with those girls, whose figures
were excessive. I was more like Eve—slim-hipped
and with high round breasts like apples, if you'll
pardon the expression. Eve never ate another
in her life, stuck with the pomegranates
even though they're the devil to peel, and bleed

that sticky juice all over your hands and thighs
as you kneel in the kitchen part of the cave.
She liked the hundreds of shiny seeds,
which she sprinkled on salads, despite Adam's
complaint that they always stuck in his teeth.
When Cain and Abel were little happy boys
they discovered the dried fruit was good
for rolling and tossing; also it was fun
to take a large stone and smash one, watching
the insides spill out into the dust. I told Eve
I didn't think it was a game to be encouraged.

She said that was the way boys always played,
though I don't know how she knew that, so
we changed the subject and I started the boys
running races to the nearest tree and back.
Adam came home soon after, I remember,
covered in dusty sweat, digging stick over shoulder,
and the races gave way to three-way wrestling.
They all looked happy, so I left. I heard
Adam as I walked away from the cave:
What do you two find to talk about every day?

When a bear

stands before you
on the lakeside trail you decided to take
as a leg-stretching walk between arriving
at the hotel and trying out the restaurant,
you stop all of a sudden at the curve
in the track and murmur *bear*
to your following husband.
He closes the gap between himself
and you, and throws one arm—
protectively or for solidarity in danger—
over your shoulder. As a pair
you offer a bulk more equal to the bear's,
though who knows this grizzly's weight
in the dappled late-afternoon gloom
under the trees?

A mutual stare
takes place across the twenty-five feet
parting your four eyes from the bear's two—
acknowledgment of otherness, if not threat
or peril. Signs warn *You are in bear country*
and pamphlets advise noisy behavior
when hiking. Singing is encouraged.
We do not sing, but look and listen,
not ready to make the first move,
so we hear a rustling in the brush, tell
each other to stand still, or even stiller.

Sure enough another bear
emerges onto the trail, something between
cub and yearling, following the mother,
as we now know her to be, across the path
onto the lake side of the track. They may,
like us, have a fish dinner in mind.

The young one climbs, then unclimbs
a dead tree—display of bravado
or exuberance, or on mother's orders
in reaction to our intrusion. The pair
wander on into the woods and vanish.
We lament our lack of a camera
on this short hike, then reconsider—
a flash might have been just
the inter-species irritant to avoid,
and we won't forget that stare.

Duo

The piano draws all significant sound in the room
into itself, asserts a key, a rhythm, a mood.

The soprano sax breaks in, swoops above,
dives, then hovers and holds the chords, the runs
in its sights; moves with the progressions.

The man at the piano is entranced, undistractable,
plays inside the music, eyes closed at times.

The woman with the sax uncoils, sways,
mesmerized and compelling, a dancer
pulled by the moves of her partner, and pulling

in her turn. She forms curlicues in the air
with the end of the instrument, makes adjustments

in the melody, the beat. He sits silent, listening,
then makes his move; turns in a new direction,
leads where she will follow.

| Four

Startled

I'd driven half a mile, not very fast,
when something on my windshield startled me:
clinging between the wipers was a mouse—no!
a bunch of mice hunched down against the wind.
There was a mother and two half-grown young,
one almost sliding up the pane of glass
but hanging on from instinct as I slowed
the car and watched the mother's bead-bright eyes
slitted against the blowing air, and then
opening to check her babies. When I could
I pulled into a dirt-paved stopping place,
got out and found a stout stick on the ground,
and pushed the mother. As she moved she pulled
her babies with her, fastened to her teats,
and one was still attached as she jumped down;
fetching the other quickly to her side
she scampered off with them into the hedge.

I thought of John Clare's sonnet "Field-Mouse's Nest"
and checked it when I came back to my desk:
I found a ball of grass among the hay
And progged it as I passed and went away...
When out an old mouse bolted in the wheat
With all her young ones hanging at her teats.
Clare's lines made me a fellow to his find
and to his wonder, though he didn't share
the driver's fright that sharpened my account.
On either side the glass the mice and I
encountered fear and had a stranger day.

No Fairytale

Driving in the dark in late November
past fallen leaves heaped in the gutter
and stacked at the roadside, I startle
when a small frog jumps into the road.

It should be too late in the season—
amphibians have bedded themselves
under flannel sheets of mud, awaiting
an ice blanket and a featherbed of snow.

But the miniature buddha's profile
lit by my highbeams is unmistakable
and I swerve. Alas, it's too dark to see
in the rearview mirror if it survived

to face more traffic, hungry owls,
earth too hard to tunnel into,
desiccating wind, and the wintry absence
of bored princesses playing in the woods.

Life in It

the cat is playing with a new toy
a small bird on the garden path

even from here I can see it's shabby
shineless and unresistant—no need

to leap and intervene   when
I search gloved in a plastic bag

under the fading begonias
I find the bird again and scoop it

but before I can reverse the gauntlet
I see movement and almost drop it

stubby grey maggots worm in and out
of the greeny-gold feathers—this finch

must have flown into the clear
glass of the new kitchen window

and broken its neck   it made
a fine new toy for the small cat

who enjoys playing with something
that still has some life in it

Sea Otters

Up the length of the coastline
        —the indented, the piney islanded—
the sea otter makes its return

now trappers aren't collecting thousands of pelts in a season,
        sea kayakers and surfers more common
        in the small beach towns,
and the old trading posts closed and forgotten.

Kelp beds flourish around and between the rocks,
throwing up specimens on the stretches of sand—
        bull kelp fifteen feet long
coiled like dead serpents, buzzing with tiny flies.

I've read how otters make daybeds of the seaweed,
        sway on its tangles in the quieter coves,
        use rocks to crack sea urchins on their chests
like opening boiled eggs at breakfast.

The fishermen never wanted the urchins
        until Japanese sushi appetites showed them a market.
Now they relish the return of eagles
who might harass the otters back into scarcity.

Feeling otherwise, I scan
the bobbing kelp bladders, gaze in hope of spotting
        something that moves independent of the waves.

An otter sighting would be my prize for the day.

The fox came back

not the very next day
but not long after the last visit we witnessed.

There had been interim crossings of the lawn—
shown by tracks on the snow
and the scrabbled spot outside my window
where he (or she) had dug
in search of a mouse, a vole, a quick
warm-blooded dinner.

Now, over the faded grass
she (or he) came trotting purposefully
from behind the garden shed
to the trodden path through the ivy
into the next yard
and the den under a privet bush—
tossed sandy dirt heaped up beside a hole.

The fox isn't red, not even auburn,
but a kind of tawny brown
accented by those black gloves (or boots)
on all four paws.

Like a pedestrian commuter
sure of the quickest route to the destination—
no hesitation, no turning aside,
nothing nervous or sly,
nothing sexy, or even suggestive.
Forget the meaning of "foxy."

Light Thrown on Winter Twigs

In my west-facing dining room
there's always a moment in the afternoon
when the sun—if there's any sun that day—
shines over the table and through
whatever flowers I have in the tall green
square glass vase.

This week it's a bunch of twigs
I clipped from the forsythia bush
that sprawls next to the washing line
by the garden shed. They were brown
and winter-dormant ten days ago,
but the buds broke

after two days in the warm house
and now they blaze yellow
as summer butter, especially
when the low sun backlights them.
The surprise of stained-glass.

No View

In fog, the brain persuades the eye
that it's looking at ocean's edge, rearing up
out of what must be the Pacific's fierce expanse,
not peaceful here, not now, as signs proclaim:
Sharks, Undertow, Trick Currents,
but under the duvet of sea-fog, breakers appear
too high, and tumble out of invisibility, fling
sand from the seabed onto a winter beach
shadowed in mid-afternoon dusk, except
when the disk of sun gleams through,
regardable as the moon, lighting the fog uncannily,
as sunshine used to push through mother's sheets
hanging to dry above the dooryard.

So years ago, climbing to Fiesole on another foggy day,
we looked back at Florence and were baffled
by the sunlit Duomo squatting high above the city
like a hen on a nest of cloud—too big to be possible
at this distance, unimaginable but indisputable,
a vision at odds with the conclusion
of the old man sitting on a low wall,
watching our reaction, commenting only on the weather,
not quite as he said: *Niente panorama.*

The Shortest Way

Desire lines, or pathways of desire,
so named by architects and planners
are those paths that appear
where no-one planned them—across
campus lawns, between
the backs of row-houses, lopping
off corners, shortcutting
to the grade-school's entrance.

If yours is the corner lot
whose lawn is trampled and trod
to a compacted trail
no seed will penetrate, consider
instead of being maddened by it,
a row of paving stones, acceding
to the majority vote. How
democratic, how neighborly.

Coming Together

I like the corners of fields
and the meeting of hedges
or drystone walls. Here
we have imposed on wildness
but nature fights back. The crop
can't grow right into the corner
so there's a small wilderness
of weeds or mud or dusty earth
a triangle beyond cultivation
where the wheat thins out
the cabbages are sparse and puny
or the hay grows lush
beyond the combine's reach.
Hedges assert their claim
in a shadowy tangle of twigs
and branches. Walls provide
hints of ancient impulses
territorial and protective:
two walls coming together
can measure boundaries
or be half a room. Sit
back to warm stone on sunlit turf
hearing the wind behind the wall
and search the sky for that lark
whose song peals down the air.

unreadable messages

in the muddy corners of the lawn
trails left by mice or voles leave hieroglyphics
that the initiated can read as tales
of tunneling under feet of snow

uncovered now and open to the sky
like wartime bomb sites that display
dangling bits of rooms clinging high
to walls held up by next-door houses

a mantel here supported by the brick
chimney column that still seems to smoke
though the rubble-dust explains the sick
smell and choking thickness of the air

no furnishings of life left on the lawn
no pile of seeds or fluff-lined nest
to show where timid eyes at dusk or dawn
scanned the snowfield for safety or peril

have the little rodents built the same
pattern of runways underneath the ground
or was the snow tunneling a sort of game
their winter sport and seasonal exercise

Countryside Map

Wall, field, wall, meadow, wall
falling down into a stony muddle
of briars and nettles. Will anyone
summon energy and motivation
to build it up again? Does it really
matter? Sheep do not graze here
any more, safely or in danger
of wandering onto the road. Hay
fills the meadow, wheat and oil-
seed rape the fields. Green turns
to gaudy yellow, umber, dun. On
the wall-stones blackberries ripen.
Children do not pick them now,
only hedge-sparrows, thrushes.

Old hawthorns stand in line
frothing white, then chopped
back by machines, torn, mutilated.
Nobody lays them into hedges
woven neat and tight as bird-nests
above straight-cut ditches. Knacks
have been lost. And there are
pseudo-hedges where barbed-wire
fences gave birds perching hold
to shit out berry seeds in rows.
Time passed. Bushes and creepers
in roadside ranks overgrew and hid
the posts and wires that propped
them. Blackthorn, holly, elder, ivy.

Florida

Roseate spoonbills put down onto the water,
stunning among the pelicans and cormorants—
yes, like rose petals dropped from the blue,
wade in the shallows, fishing by feel, scooping
side-to-side with their—yes, soup-spoon bills.

Dunlins and dowitchers stitch the sandbar,
clockwork mice crossed with sewing machines,
tireless, unimpressed by dazzling egret plumes
and unlikely yellow feet, tangerine ibis beaks,
dignity of herons' slow scholarly stepping.

They see these every day. We point and gloat
over new knowledge, distinctions made clear
by our books and binoculars. But after all,
the pleasure lies in nothing that can be listed,
entered, checked. It is the homing glide

of pelicans before they turn awkward, beak-
heavy, when their almost square webbed feet
unfold like landing-gear, legs spread to break
the hard blue water. It is the cormorants' wings
hung out to dry, black amid the commotion.

Water Windflower

Low tide. The sea anemone:
a blind nubbin hidden among weed fronds,
hugs itself to itself, waiting for the tide to turn.
At the water's first touch its rubbery surface gleams;
with the next few waves it swells and softens.
As the water fills the pool with its suck and surge
the anemone opens; tentacles emerge, one by one at first,
then the rest at once, like the flames on a reluctant gas jet.
It sways with the wash of the waves
and with its own sensations. It clings
to whatever's introduced to it;
a child's exploring finger
feels minuscule suckers inside each smooth-looking arm.
Transparent shrimp
cannot spring backward fast enough to escape;
hatchling fish
seeking the shelter of surrounding weeds
don't stand a chance if they graze the greedy petals:
this is the sensitive plant of the animal world. It seizes,
swallows, digests; then spits out its tiny leavings.
The sun, or the moon, crosses the sky. Waves caress,
or crash through the pool, scouring it with salty sand.
The anemone clings on.
At the turn of the tide it sucks itself a kiss,
shrinks to its minimum, a button
of inanimate jelly, and waits.

Orbis Muscae

One of those tiny silent flies
with iridescent head and eyes
is showing a fascination
for my globe, no particular nation
unless it's perhaps Ghana,
which Sam smeared with banana
this morning after his snack.
The fly keeps coming back
to Africa from other places,
and may until no further traces
of sticky sweetness remain.
It's like a gaudy little plane
flown by one of those dictators
who likes to claim it caters
to the naïve expectations
of his and nearby populations.
The fly's less likely, though,
to be sabotaged and blow
to fragments between one dust-
powdered forgotten outpost
and another. I have no reason
to squash it out of season.
Were he here, Sam might try—
not so much to see it die
as because it's fragile, shiny,
moving, within his reach, and tiny.

Perfect Arcs

When the bough breaks is when it's bent too far
beyond its natural bow, the one akin to a curtsey
or a kowtow, courtesy required of the courtiers of Cathay.

But the strongbow, the longbow, even the bow you tie
around your neck, in your daughter's hair, or on a gift box,
this is the one related to the rainbow, the sky arch, the *arc-en-ciel*

which we tie in our minds to the place where it first appeared,
in story at any rate, Mount Ararat. It's inextricable
from the other kind of ark, of gopher wood measured out in cubits.

How different from the Greeks' version of Iris
goddess of the shimmering robes, the beguiling look
of sunshine on wet garments. She knew the other meaning of arch

and no doubt always kept her eyebrows plucked into perfect arcs.
She would have made a good figurehead, carved into the bow
of a wooden craft bent to just the wave-cutting curve.

Five

Surfacing

...a nose perfume old father de crabs
ancient essence of ocean, of tideline, of wrack,
salt and rot and things churned to the sand's surface
by wave and wind, delving gull and tern and piping plover

even a sandcastle spade sometimes turns up
stinks that need to be covered quickly, the castle reseated—
here bones of dogfish, still linked by cartilage, recognizable
from the biology lab dissecting table

there a wingful of feathers and four vertebrae, stuck together
with organic cement, sand and connective tissue bonded
and now insoluble as jeweler's glue or dentist's amalgam
or the horse-hoof melted to the shoe

down the beach, entangled in kelp and greener weed
a crab shell hollowed out by pecking birds and buzzing flies
parodies the treat in the crab shack beyond the dunes
with sides of slaw and fries, tartar sauce from a jar

...so much from a string of words marooned by a dream on awakening

Dream Strangers

Who was that woman in my dream
in the soft coat she so suddenly opened
to surprise us with her nakedness?
She was slender, tall, not quite flat-chested
(her breasts were adolescent nubbins)
and daubed with white sunscreen
in the places where she'd worn a bikini
(did she want to keep those parts pale?)

And where do the strangers in our dreams
come from? Have we glimpsed them
in the street, the mall, a restaurant,
and registered their faces for future use?
What of the people who live in places
without hordes of strangers to draw on—
dwellers in mountain villages
where all the populace is familiar,

inhabitants of monasteries, communes,
rainforest settlements, where strangers
never come? Do they make dream characters
by jigsawing together bits and pieces
of the people they know? Maybe that's
what we all do, when we need strangers
in our dreams, when parents, friends, enemies
even, will not suffice for what has to be done.

Under Three Skies

Full moonlight exaggerates the newly bare trees.
I think of running with a dog for miles. Cold. Sweating
and panting both. Stars swing over the black bowl above.
Where are we going?

                **

Winds have thrown down branches and bits of branches,
one with a point stuck upright in the muddy lawn.
I dream a bonfire, cooking things on sticks or in the embers—
sausages, potatoes—back to childhood.

                **

The beach at sunset is returned to the birds. Gulls pick up
after messy picnickers, peck at eggshells, bottle caps.
Flocks of small waders chase and are chased by the waves,
quick legs scissoring the red water.

Night Cries

Little foxes and young owls
make small yips and wheeps
at the smell of blood. They
are excited by warm furry
gobbets of flesh and bone.
They fight their siblings
for them, then luxuriate
in snapping and crunching
every last scrap. This is
one reason the countryside
isn't overrun with mice. If
these youngsters refused
such messy treats, or gagged
at food that still sometimes
wriggles against the palate
or shrieks when shared out,
they'd soon starve and die.

English poems use the cry
of the owl to call up darkness,
cold and melancholy;
the bark of the fox stands
for wildness. A winter
landscape, scraped bare,
looks inhospitable to life,
but the predators love it
when every rustle
in the stilled hedgerow,
every darting shadow
means a dinner-morsel.

Long and Winding Yarn

My grandchild wants to learn to knit,
so I find big needles and leftover wool,
cast on fifteen stitches and show her
the moves my fingers know by heart,
breaking them into steps I can describe
in words: *poke, wind, catch, and push.*
She and I work together, my fingers
enclosing hers and guiding the yarn,
the needles, and her eager hands. She
names the motions as she makes them
until I feel she grasps the trick of it, let
her try the ancient skill all by herself.
She likes to hear that *knit* and *knot*
are versions of the same word, sees
the little row of knots she's making,
she and the needles, with each row.
Her brother appears, watches awhile,
and whispers to me *She's talking to
her knitting.* A good sign—she knows
it already has existence, even though
it's no more than three inches long. It
will be a scarf for their youngest cousin
in time for Christmas, they determine.
I tell them the first knitters lived many
thousands of years ago. We imagine
the first vest, the knotted fishing nets.
Just this week the paper reported that
textiles were found in Spanish caves,
twisted yarns that pushed this craft's
beginning back by thousands of years.
I tell the grandchildren my mother,
their English granny, was the knitter
of socks, gloves, patterns I never tried.
They don't need to hear about her last
sweater, left in an unfinished muddle
for someone to rescue and complete.
It came to me. I wear it and feel warm.

The Russian doll I played with as a child

split open to present another doll just like its mother
who split in turn, and so on to eight generations,
with the last, innermost, baby the size of a bean.
It had become an infant, naked, too small
to play with, unsplittable.

All it could do was take its place in the line
of its reassembled ancestors, who did,
like the real grown women we knew,
wear slightly different clothes,
though all of a kind.

All had gaily painted babushkas
covering head and shoulders,
even when too small for
embroidered flowers.

All had aprons, although
at last they were only
vertical splashes
of white paint.

All had black stares,
small red smiles,
split bellies.

I didn't know, then,
quite how real human babies
came out of their mother's tummies,
that it was a different kind of splitting,

but I had the same shivery feeling as when
a book had the tricky sort of picture on the cover
that showed the child in the book reading the same book,
with the same picture, only smaller, and so on for ever and ever.

Someone could have told me,
even then, that the dolls were true to life:
the tier of generations, age-old teetering balance
between same and new. One mother then another making the miracle
of splitting and continuing, passing on the matter that keeps us recognizable.

Night Thoughts Organized

When I lie awake and need to turn my mind away
from the fret-of-the-day
I sometimes try to tread
a path that doesn't detour from a well-worn thread
through the forest of my fret:
I organize my drifting thoughts along the alphabet.

It could be birds, or flowers, or poets, rivers, trees,
cities in Europe, even arthropods, including fleas.
Last night I tried to list the things I took to college—
afghan, books, coffee mugs—but my knowledge
of the room was strangely blurred.
My belongings seemed to have been stirred
into the mess of what I've owned since then—
a typewriter superimposed on the trusty fountain pen
with which I wrote my essays and exams
(we all did in 'sixties England, between showing off our gams
in miniskirts and bare skin, or else in fishnet tights,
when sallying forth for nights
at the cinema or pub, or in some bloke's room or other,
some of whom would not have charmed my mother).

The *dictionary* I won at school,
eyeshadow to make me look cool,
when I wore those *fishnet tights* and rode my bike
into town, before the days of bike locks, so I had to hike
back to college by midnight when the bike was taken
from the railings I leant it against, mistaken
in thinking it was safe amongst the line
of other bikes; why would a thief take mine?

I wore stockings and a *girdle* too, with those suspender hooks
that were supposed to rivet the looks
of girl-hungry students who got our dresses off.
I remember one young toff...
But more innocently there were *handkerchiefs,* a cotton

stack of them ready for when I had a rotten
cold (we didn't use tissues then) or spilled my *ink*—
on my desk there was always a bottle of royal blue Qink
and nearby a jar or two of *jam,* carefully brought from home,
standing on a different shelf from my brush and comb.
My mind wanders to the word "unkempt"
wondering if its opposite, "kempt"
could let me cheat and use the Old Norse *kambr,*
descended, the dictionary shows, like a fly in amber
from the Greek for tooth (but this root of the ancient word
would, honestly, not have occurred
to me, sleepless, in the night
but had to wait until the following morning's light).

My *letter-writing* set—paper, envelopes, stamps—was not
put to much use; my parents were lucky if they got
news from me every fortnight, and then only selected
highlights of such activities as I elected
to report: a punting picnic, choir concert I sang in,
the May Day morning celebrations when all the bells rang in
the spring, and foolish students jumped into the river at dawn...
And here I yawn
before reaching even the middle of the alphabet—
nothing for a simple letter like M yet...

Many Applicants for One-Way Travel to Mars

New York Times, Dec. 9, 2014

If there's life on Mars
It's a smidgen
Not as complex
As even a pigeon

It's just a dot
Of chemical potential
Not even a spot
To which I can feel reverential

But there are people
Who strongly desire
To travel in a spaceship
Beyond the moon, higher

And farther and colder,
Into a place of no return.
They are either stupider or bolder
Than I, who absolutely do not yearn

For existence whittled down
To survival on a planet bare
Of plants, birds, strangers in town,
Good food. Don't send me there.

Mother Goose Mash-Up

Miss Muffet sat in the cobwebby corner
Where Jack abandoned the pie
After he picked out the plums.
She watched the spider wrap a fly.

*

The boy in blue let the sheep
Get into the cornfield and make a mess
While he sat by the haystack
Unbuttoning the shepherdess.

*

The old woman in the shoe
Said upon her life
She'd rather live in a pumpkin
Like that rascal Peter's wife.

*

I had a little pony
Nothing would it bear
But the King of Spain's daughter
Naked and bare.

A ring on every finger
Silver nutmegs on her toes
And a tiny golden pear
At the side of her nose.

She skipped over water
Like a white pebble-stone
And brought me a nut tree
All my own.

Look Again

The king was in the kitchen
eating bread and honey
The maid was in the office
counting up the money
The queen was in the laundry
waiting on the clothes
and flipping through a magazine
in search of a new nose

Before and after pictures
showed what could be done
She thought a little button nose
would be kind of fun
or else something more Roman
might excite the king
even a Grecian profile
could be just the thing

The clown was in the White House
trying to read a book
when in swooped a news cam
for an unbelieving look
Yes it was just as it seemed
the yellow-headed clown
could not make head nor tail of it
the book was upside-down

| Six

The White Horse at Uffington, Oxfordshire

Deformed by the slash-and-basketweave
of ancient hedge-laying
twisted hawthorns centuries old
mark field boundaries and lane edges.

Above them lies the chalky pastureland
crisscrossed by sheep tracks
studded with flint-hearted clods
that split to shine with bruise tints.

If you take two chunks and clash them
together like cymbals
you can sniff the fire in the rock
different from the smell of wood-smoke.

When they cut the horse into the hill
the running horse spirit
white against green grass and clover
they still used flints to make fire.

Turf hillocks around the white horse
fold it into the slope
protect it with meandering paths
to other stretches of thyme and harebells

mounded into long barrows for burial
or tumuli with unknown uses
and mystified names from later ages
George and the Dragon or Alfred's Castle.

Beeches around one barrow were graven
with pairs of initials

by people who came along this valley
when the railway was the iron horse.

Under a slanting light at dawn or dusk
the land has ripples
like a place where waves or wind
have worked the surface over and over.

Naming Wildflowers

They used to know the flowers so closely,
named them as they did each other: Carpenter
or Stout, nicknames for everyday helpful use.
Accordingly there's *cranesbill*, showing the shape
of the wild geranium's seed head, or *monkshood*,
blue delphinium of the woods, with the flower's
extended tube like the liripipe that hangs down the back
in medieval costume. *Birdsfoot trefoil*, yellow as summer
butter when the cows have rich grazing, has three-way leaves
and triple seedpods, splayed like a bird's toes
as it walks the dust. Old roads and new highways
are edged with its gleaming. Its cousin, *butter-and-eggs*,
has the pale golden crumpled look of a good breakfast scramble,
and *cleavers* sticks to the clothes of passersby to spread itself.

There are flowers named whimsically: *foxglove* and *harebell*,
and others for their properties. As children we learned
to recognize *deadly nightshade* with its poisonous berries,
and half-believed that *dock* was short for "doctor"
and could soothe a nettle's sting if rubbed on it
quickly enough. We'd left behind the knowledge
that *feverfew* was a cure-all, and (not yet knowing French)
had to have explained that the fine-cut foliage of *fumitory*
growing up the wall looked like smoke climbing a chimney,
and that the *dandelion's* jagged leaves had reminded
someone of a lion's teeth. Today we're told to protect
wildflowers by leaving them alone—no more picking them,
pressing them, mounting them in albums, noting the date
we found them. We treat them like faces in a crowd, not friends.

Dodder [n.]

Who did in the dodder
or did it just give up
its stranglehold
on the bankside weeds
beside the canal?

In spring it ups and clings
to stuff with straight stems
a spaghetti clutch
on a greedy fork.

It seems mindful
bent on smothering its hosts
yet it dithers and dangles
its floppy parasitical tresses
in shapeless copper tangles
aimless complications.

Late summer finds it
        gone
                not a sign
to be seen
on the standing weeds.

If by spores
or some other
        secret reproductive means
it may reappear in its season
        for now it seems
the dodder is dead.

Witch Hazel

At the tag-end of winter
or the first hint of spring
sometimes the air holds
promise of something
other than snow—a hint
of fragrance in the cold
drizzle-burdened air.

Look around and find
the source—over there
the yellow of lemon rind
all along the twigs
of a small wayside tree—
tiny crumpled rags
like left-behind prayers
from a band of the Wee
Folk.

A good witch could use
the hazel sap to heal
a rash or a bruise
and its power was real—
not just talk.

Nettles

Our mother sometimes fed us on scrag end—
the worst part of a sheep's neck, bone and gristle,
though the butcher insisted it was lamb, saying
only the Scots (he could tell from her accent)
asked him for mutton. Stewed long enough
the meat became edible, though not tender,
and made a rich gravy.
                                    Mum was proud
of her Scottish ancestry, would tell us the legend
of that country's heraldic flower, the thistle:
how a band of English marauders tried to attack
the rocky crag crowned by Edinburgh Castle
but in the dark one of them laid hold on the plant
with its fierce array of thorns, and shouted out
at the pain, alerting the Scots in their stronghold.

And I liked the verse about Simple Simon
going to see *if plums grew on a thistle*
only to experience the same harsh pain
which made poor Simon whistle.
When we walked in the fields we knew
to watch out for thistles and stinging nettles
with their minuscule but deadly bristles.

Under the Skin

Golden ball,
seamed and crazed
by sun and soil,
fat now and able
only to loll
under its vine
awaiting the pull
and twist
that today will
bring it to harvest
and fulfill
its sweet destiny,
put it in goal.

It will be sniffed,
thumbed, squeezed,
masking its heft
behind its crust,
a seeming thrift
that veils prodigal
delights with deft
dignity, undone
only when cleft
with a knife.
Then its wet, soft
insides display
the fecund raft
of precious seeds.
Such craft,
to cradle in luscious
flesh its final gift.

Pole Beans

Poking beans into the earth I still mutter
what I taught my son as he helped with the planting:
One for the mouse, one for the crow,
One to rot and one to grow.
But days later each pole has three sprouting beans.
I should choose the sturdiest and uproot the rest
but I prefer to let them fight it out,
picturing a tangle of leaves and scarlet flowers.
Only they wander so, drifting in all directions
and I want to help them climb, but
I can't recall how they twine—clockwise
or widdershins. Twisting them the wrong way
will slow their ascent, confuse the corkscrew.
I must wait for the fastest to show me what to do.

Unchanged

That same tumbled strand of creeping vine—
the one trailing crimson from the phone wire—
was hanging over a riverside bluff in China
three hundred years ago. I've seen it
in an ink painting where each leaflet
was executed with a single brushstroke,
fuller or lighter as size and position required,
the painter flicking and turning the tuft
of squirrel hairs embedded in bamboo,
then laying his wrist on its porcelain rest.
Later, beside the cliff and dangling creeper
he painted his poem in flowing characters:
>   The vine hangs over the rock
>   Water mirrors new and old
>   The scholar sits on the riverbank.

Winter Trees Are Like Pencil Sketches

This line opened an essay in the *Reader's Digest*
I read in a waiting room decades ago. It persuaded me—
through its concision, its vividness, its rhythm—
of its truth, if a simile can be said to be true. The rest
of the essay has slipped my mind, though I can guess
it spoke of the spring and summer watercolors or oils
that fill in with green these monochrome drawings,
blurring the outlines of twigs and branches until
we can't see the trees for the forest. Probably
the author described how clearly we can distinguish
one leaf-bare tree from another—the low and level
branches of the beech, often still clinging to last year's
brown and battered leaves, the upward-stretching ash,
the intricate patterning of oak and maple boughs—
and how, with the fudge-factor of foliage gone,
trees are as clear as architects' drawings, no room
for decorative distractions like color, cornices, tile-work.
The artist takes responsibility for line, balance, weight
and whatever gives each tree its knowable character,
that which distinguishes it from its neighbor, or
from the lollipop blobs—brown trunks, green leaves—
of children's paintings. I yearn to be the sketcher
and to get each winter tree just right.

Nothing

this is a poem about nothing
the nothing of me before I was born
the nothing after my death

the nothing Cordelia inherited
out of her "Nothing"
except all her father's love

the nothing a naughty child
has been up to
when a parent wants to know

the nothing I had on
under my jeans
when I answered the door at 7 a.m.

the nothing left of a father's voice
of a mother's curious glance
when you told her nothing

the nothing you can do
with the hundreds of family photos
four and five generations deep

the nothing you can remember
on the shopping list
you left in the kitchen

the nothing that makes sense
in the dark of your bed
when sleep defies your yearning

the nothing I said
sotto voce
when no-one was supposed to hear

The Work of a Poet

Here is the *makar* of Scotland, the crafter
of words, the one who creates out of nothing,
out of anything, something new: a song
or a murmur of words that stand in shape
and mean themselves afresh.

And here the *wright,* now always tag-end
of a term: wheelwright, cartwright, playwright,
the one who wrought, perhaps from iron
or from wood, or both in turn,
or out of words, gestures, actions, a story.

There, in Afghanistan, a man who does both,
works in metal and in Pashtun—a poet.
Matiullah Turab tells what he does:
Banging iron, cutting it short, making it long
the way a poem's lines are made.

The Persistence of Myopia in the Human Gene-Pool

They shouldn't have survived to reproduce, surely,
those who couldn't see clearly beyond the cave mouth,
couldn't be sure if that was a bear or a horse approaching
across the slope in front of the forest. Useless at hunting,
they couldn't read the silent signals saying *Back up,* or
Circle left or *Charge!* They sometimes hailed
members of an enemy band, ignored a bigwig coming
to the home-place in a visit of honor. They didn't know
hawk from gull on the wind, hare from fox in the grass.

But when it came to the skinning of game, the detail
work around joints and jawbones, they wielded knives
with astounding skill. They could tell which tree-bark
cured headache, which seedpod soothed colic
in a crying child or a toothless ancient weak of digestion.
They chose among gathered plants the ones to throw
on the midden lest all be poisoned, picked out
the birds' eggs that shouldn't be taken again, because
the breed was thinning, their songs scarcely heard.

And they had their own songs, made in the quiet
of the empty cave deserted by hunters and foragers.
They spoke of the fear that was a feather on the spine,
the content that came from skin next to skin at night
or sun on still water, moonlight on snowpack.
They passed on tales of wanderings, encounters, clashes
in family and clan, of battle and blood, war triumph,
success in the hunt. A whittled bone made a flute
for piercing melody. It lay long-buried with the maker.

| Acknowledgments

Grateful acknowledgment to the editors of the magazines in which some of the poems in this book first appeared: "Nothing," "Pole Beans," and "No View" in *U.S. 1 Worksheets*; "Perfect Arcs" in *Anon One*; "At the Bungalow" in the *New Yorker*.

In memory of the parents who gave me my first love of poetry, and the teachers who nurtured it. And with thanks to all my poet friends and supporters, to Ellen Foos, excellent editor, to Larry Danson, without whom this book would never have seen the light of day, and to the rest of my family, encouraging as ever.

| About the Author

Elizabeth Danson's first memories are of an early childhood in China. She was educated in England and has spent her adult life in the United States.

For many years she taught, both children and adults; more recently worked for a publisher and a local arts center; and has published essays and poems on both sides of the Atlantic.

www.ingramcontent.com/pod-product-compliance
Lightning Source LLC
Chambersburg PA
CBHW020946090426
42736CB00010B/1293